MARVEL
HEROES

MIX
Paper from
responsible sources
FSC® C005461

Marvel Heroes Annual 2019 is published by Panini Publishing, a division of Panini UK Limited. Office of publication: Panini UK Ltd. Brockbourne House, 77 Mount Ephraim, Tunbridge Wells, Kent, TN4 8BS. MARVEL, and all related characters: TM & © 2018 Marvel Entertainment, LLC and its subsidiaries. Licensed by Marvel Characters B.V. www.marvel.com. All rights reserved. No similarity between any of the names, characters, persons and/or institutions in this edition with those of any living or dead person or institution is intended, and any such similarity which may exist is purely coincidental. This publication may not be sold, except by authorised dealers, and is sold subject to the condition that it shall not be sold or distributed with any part of its cover or markings removed, nor in a mutilated condition. This publication is produced under licence from Marvel Characters, Inc. through Panini S.p.A. Printed in Italy by Rotolito S.p.A. ISBN: 978-1-84653-240-5

© 2018 MARVEL

£7.99

Across the universe, there are countless cosmic villains who want to rule over Earth! Make no mistake - these intergalactic invaders are some of the Avengers' deadliest enemies!

KANG THE CONQUEROR

A time-travelling tyrant from the distant future of the 31st century, Kang doesn't just want to rule the universe - he wants to rule all of time! Constantly changing his appearance over the years, there's no telling where (or when) Kang will strike next!

REAL NAME
Nathaniel Richards

BASE OF OPERATION
Chronopolis

NOTABLE ALIASES
• Pharoah Rama-Tut
• The Scarlet Centurion
• Immortus
• Iron Lad

MICHAEL KORVAC

Michael Korvac is an unbelievably powerful energy-harnessing cyborg from an alternate version of history. Able to attack his enemies with hazardous amounts of cosmic radiation, Korvac was even once able to bring Galactus to his knees!

PLACE OF ORIGIN
The Blue Area of Earth's moon, Luna – in another version of our universe

COSMIC POWERS
In his cyborg form, Korvac is able to weaponise any form of energy – solar radiation, heat, x-rays... you name it!

NOTABLE ALIASES
• The Bright Lord
• Jaboa Murphy

PLANET OF ORIGIN
Hala, Pama System, the Kree Empire

ACCUSER'S ABILITIES
Ronan's exceptional hand-to-hand combat skills are boosted by superhuman strength and endurance

TYRANNICAL TECH
• Exoskeleton armour
• Ronan's multifunctioning Universal Weapon

CONQUERORS

THANOS

Thanos, the Mad King of Saturn's moon, is perhaps the most dangerous tyrant the Avengers have ever encountered! Embarking on numerous quests to eliminate Earth - all he really cares about is impressing the fearsome Lady Death!

PLACE OF ORIGIN

Titan, the largest moon of Saturn

TYRANNICAL TECH

Thanos seeks to regain the Infinity Gems, hoping to harness their almighty power within the Infinity Gauntlet

POWERS

- Vast superhuman strength and stamina.
- Accelerated healing factor and near-immortality.
- Thanos possesses shockingly powerful telepathic abilities.

ANNIHILUS

The self-proclaimed Lord of the otherworldly Negative Zone, Annihilus is an insectoid creature who will stop at nothing to spread the horror of his homeworld.

RONAN

Ronan the Accuser is one of the most fearsome warriors in any galaxy - a legend among his Kree brethren. A judge to those who wrong the Kree, he has clashed with Earth's heroes many times.

BASE OF OPERATION

Sector 17-A of the Negative Zone

TYRANNICAL TECH

Annihilus is in possession of the Cosmic Control Rod, a devastating tool that allows him to both attack his enemies and protect himself from the Negative Zone's hostile environment.

FIGHTING FISTS

With the Infinity Gauntlet's power at his fingertips, Thanos is virtually unstoppable! But the Mad Titan isn't the only one with mighty mitts. Write the correct letters in the blank spaces below to link these heroes and villains with their fighting fists!

A. Ulysses Klaw

B. The Black Panther

C. Ultron

D. Doctor Doom

E. Black Widow

ANSWERS ON PAGE 61

"WITH THAT, ASGARD'S MAJESTY WAS RESTORED.

"ODIN, NOW THE KEEPER OF THE INFINITY GAUNTLET, USED ITS MAGIC TO REVERSE WHAT THANOS HAD DONE ON EARTH, AND LOCKED IT AWAY WITH HIS OTHER TREASURES.

"THE AVENGERS, WHO HAD RETURNED THOSE TREASURES TO THEIR RIGHTFUL HOME, WERE CELEBRATED IN THE HALLS OF VALHALLA.

"AS FOR MY PART IN THIS?"

THERE ARE SOME THINGS THAT TRANSPIRE THAT MY BRETHREN NEED NOT KNOW.

ULTIMATE POWER DOES NOT A HERO MAKE. THE TRUE POWER IS IN THE WISDOM TO USE THAT STRENGTH AS A FORCE FOR GOOD.

CAPTAIN AMERICA, IRON MAN, HULK, THOR, BLACK WIDOW, FALCON, HAWKEYE--THEY USE THEIR GIFTS TO HELP THOSE WHO CANNOT STAND UP TO EVIL THEMSELVES. THEY ARE THE HEROES.

MY DUTY IS SIMPLY TO OBSERVE.

THE END!

HOW TO DRAW THANOS

Can you draw the Mad Titan? Follow these quick steps and practise your drawing skills!

1.

Draw an oval head shape and mark in where the facial features will be.

2.

Mark in the eyes, nose and mouth in rough.

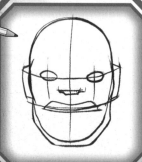

3.

Add his eyebrows and helmet lines.

4.

Finish the chin and finer parts of his face. remove any rough lines.

1.

Stick man first! Go lightly with the pencil as you'll rub this out later.

2.

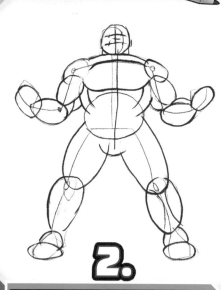

Fill out the sketch with oval shapes for the body, head and limbs.

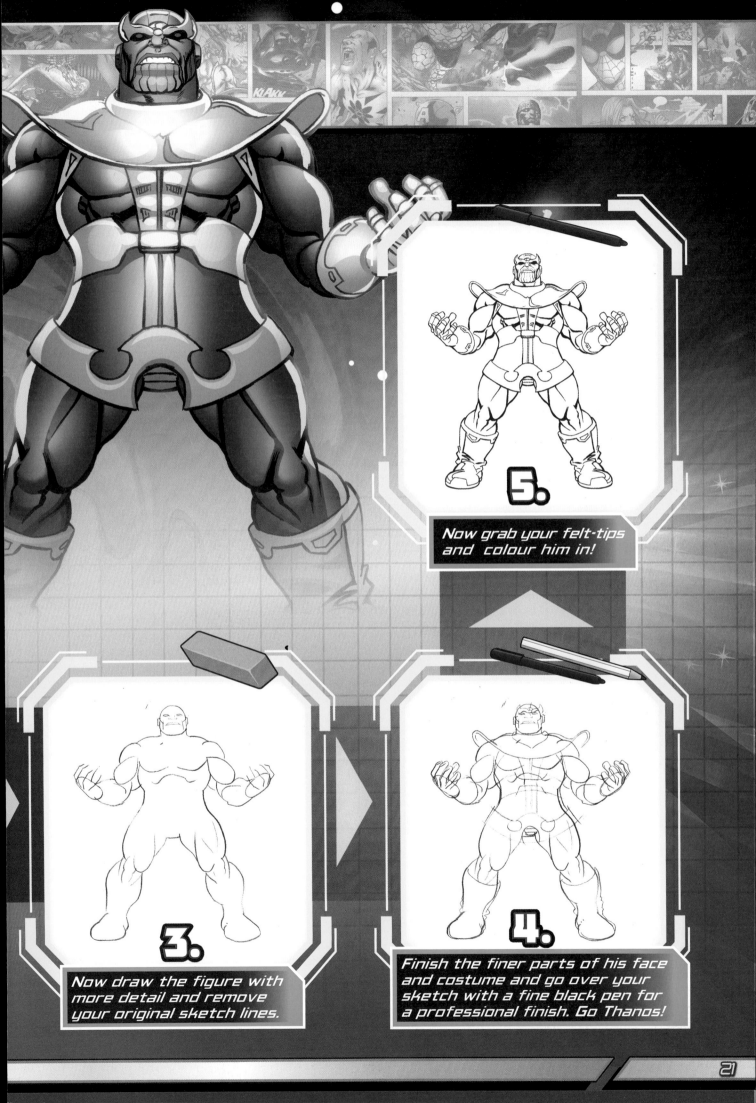

5. Now grab your felt-tips and colour him in!

3. Now draw the figure with more detail and remove your original sketch lines.

4. Finish the finer parts of his face and costume and go over your sketch with a fine black pen for a professional finish. Go Thanos!

SPELL BOUND

Dr Strange is trapped in Dormammu's cursed chains! Decode the magic phrase to set him free.

DECODER

ᛘ D	ᛒ E	ᚳ H
ᛜ N	ᛝ P	ᛞ R
ᛉ S	ᛌ T	ᚨ U

ANSWERS ON PAGE 61

MIGHTY MARVEL FUN

CITY SEARCH

Hawkeye is looking out for Chitauri warriors in the city. Can you help him spot all of the things listed below?

x1

x1

x6

x1

ROCKET'S WORKSHOP

He's a hairy, weapons-crafting, easily upset furbag of anger, and his name's **Rocket Raccoon!** Help him out with these projects before he loses it!

' ' YOU CAN'T GET THE STAFF

1. This A'askvarii shock staff is protected by a stasis field to stop the rest of the crew messing with it. But Rocket can't remember the combination!

WARM

Help him deactivate it by using the thermal imager. The coldest buttons (blue) were the first ones entered and the warm buttons (red) were the last.

1	2	3
4	5	6
7	8	9

COLD

ENTER CODE HERE ☐☐☐☐☐

MISS ME?

2.

Rocket's made so many prototypes of the beam emission blaster, he's forgotten which one was the first. Can you match it up to the original?

ORIGINAL

A.

B.

C.

D.

TARGET INCOMING

3.

Which one of these incoming craft will reach Rocket's ship first? Use the speed and distance values to work it out!

ALPHA CRAFT
Speed: 1000mph
Distance: 8 miles

CENTAURI CRUISER
Speed: 250mph
Distance: 1 mile

ROCKET'S SHIP

QUAD STRIKER
Speed: 2000mph
Distance: 10 miles

SPEED RACER
Speed: 73mph
Distance: 1000 miles

ANSWERS ON PAGE 61

ATTACK OF THE GIANTS!

FINISH!

By Odin's beard! The fearsome Frost Giants have dared to attack Asgard! Can you guide Thor safely past them to climb up to the Imperial Palace and warn his father? Speed is of the essence!

START!

ANSWERS ON PAGE 61

ASGARD ON ICE

JOE CARAMAGNA – WRITER   WELLINTON ALVES – PENCILER
ANDERSON SILVA – INKER   CARLOS LOPEZ – COLORIST   VC'S JC – LETTERING
MARK BASSO – ASSISTANT EDITOR   BILL ROSEMANN – EDITOR
AXEL ALONSO – EDITOR IN CHIEF   DAN BUCKLEY – PUBLISHER
JOE QUESADA – CHIEF CREATIVE OFFICER   ALAN FINE – EXECUTIVE PRODUCER

THERE WAS A TIME WHEN PEOPLE THOUGHT *LIGHTNING* WAS MAGIC, TOO. THEN WE LEARNED ABOUT *IONIZATION* AND POSITIVE AND NEGATIVE CHARGES.

ALL "MAGIC" IS EXPLAINED BY SCIENCE. *EVENTUALLY.*

WHAT ABOUT *YOU,* CAP? DO YOU BELIEVE IN MAGIC?

I THINK IF A PERSON REALLY *BELIEVES* HE CAN DO SOMETHING--

--AND SETS HIS *MIND* TO IT--

--ANYTHING IS POSSIBLE.

WHAT I WOULDN'T GIVE TO RUN A FULL POLYSOMNOGRAPHIC STUDY ON ODIN WHILE HE'S SLEEPING...

FORGET IT, SAM.

I DON'T BELIEVE IN MAGIC, BUT I *DO* BELIEVE HE'D KNOCK YOUR BLOCK OFF IF YOU WOKE HIM UP.

ISN'T ODIN'S PALACE THE *OTHER* WAY, THOR? WHAT IS THIS PLACE?

IF WE ARE TO DRIVE BACK OUR ATTACKERS AND RESTORE THIS KINGDOM TO ITS *GLORY,* WE MUST FREE THEIR MOST DANGEROUS *PRISONER...*

...MY BROTHER *LOKI!*

29

ARE-- ARE YOU SURE THIS IS A GOOD IDEA?

YOU KNOW HE *HATES* YOU, RIGHT?

LOKI IS THE ONE WHO SUMMONED ME WHEN ASGARD WAS ATTACKED. HE IS JUST AS INVESTED IN OUR FATHER'S KINGDOM AS I AM.

AND HE'S STILL MY *BROTHER.*

STAND BACK!

KER-*FOOM*

THUD

EVERY. SINGLE. TIME. SO *PREDICTABLE!*

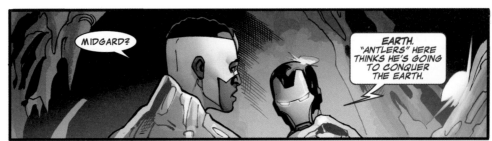

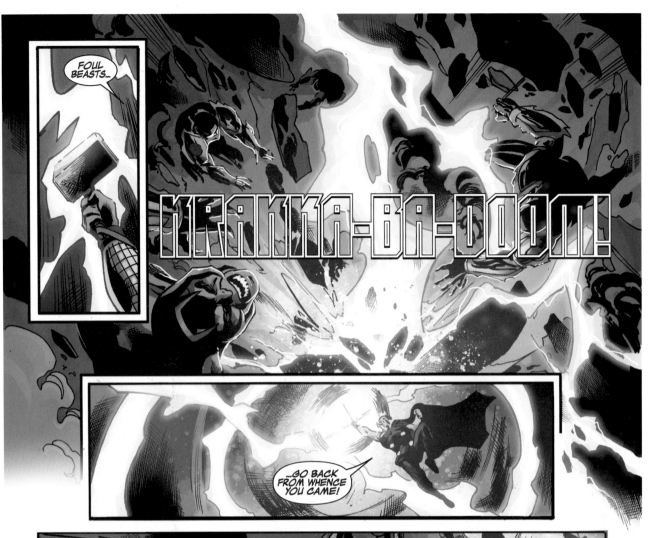

THE END!

THE NINE REALMS

Thor guides us through all the worlds of our dimension.

Nine Realms art: Haemi Jang

Vanaheim

Vanaheim is the realm of the Vanir, a race of wise and ancient beings; our Asgardian cousins. Once we warred against each other, but now we are staunch allies.

Midgard (Earth)

Home of the mortal humans who commonly refer to it as planet Earth. I was banished to Midgard to learn humility, and have defended it many times from numerous threats.

Svartalfheim

This dangerous land is home to the evil Dark Elves. They are ruled by their corrupt lord, Malekith, who once came close to conquering Asgard by using the Casket of Ancient Winters to unleash deadly snowstorms.

Niffleheim

Within this dark mist-shrouded underworld lies the foreboding ruler, Hela, Queen of the Dead. For eons she has tried to trap Thor in her kingdom, but she has always failed.

YGGDRASIL
THE WORLD TREE

VANAHEIM
HOME OF THE VANIR,
WISE GODS OF OLD

MIDGARD
THE REALM OF
MORTALS

ASGARDIA
WHERE NOW
DWELL THE GODS
OF OLD ASGARD

NIFFLEHEIM
THE FROZEN UNDERWORLD

SVARTALFHEIM
THE DARK FAERIE REALM

Asgard

Connected to Midgard (Earth) by the mystical Bifrost (Rainbow Bridge), Asgard is the greatest of all realms! For it is here that I and my friends dwell, defending the Nine Realms.

Alfheim

The beautiful realm of the equally beautiful Light Elves. But do not be deceived by their pleasant looks, as they are deadly warriors.

Nidavellir

Here dwell the dwarves and their king, Hreidmar. The dwarves are master craftsman and have forged many weapons, including Thor's mystic hammer, Mjolnir.

Jotunheim

The icy land of Jotunheim is home to the cruel Frost Giants. Many a time have I fought these vile creaures, who are always seeking to destroy Asgard.

ASGARD
WHERE ONCE
DWELT THE
GODS

ALFHEIM
REALM OF THE LIGHT ELVES

NIDAVELLIR
LAND OF THE DWARVES

JOTUNHEIM
HERE BE GIANTS

MUSPELHEIM
WHERE FIRE WAS BORN

Muspelheim

A realm of raging fire, it is ruled over by the dreaded fire demon, Surtur, who is always seeking to bring about Ragnarok - the end of the world!

DEY

Can you spot all of these characters in this epic scene? Tick them off as you find them!

VILLAINS

BONUS ROUND!

Can you also spot..?

4 Spidey Webs

1 Iron Spider Backpack

1 S.H.I.E.L.D. Tri-Carrier

4

Ant-Man has developed a brand-new batch of Pym Particles, and he'll need them for the Avengers' next mission! Race the Wasp back to Pym's lab to see which tiny titan is faster!

WHAT YOU NEED:
- A DICE
- TWO COUNTERS

USE THE PYM PARTICLES TO GET BIG AND STOP A ROBBERY! YOU'RE ON A ROLL – ADVANCE TWO SPACES!

USE YOUR WINGS AND QUICKLY GET AHEAD! FLY FORWARD TWO SPACES.

THE WASP START

4

3

5

2

6

1

7

8

9

PYM'S LAB

13

10

12

11

A CARELESS PEDESTRIAN NEARLY SWATS THE WASP! FALL BACK TWO SPACES.

OH NO! DOCTOR DOOM ATTACKS! TEAM UP WITH THE BLACK WIDOW TO TAKE HIM DOWN! GO BACK ONE SPACE.

THE WASP!

THE LAB'S ADVANCED SECURITY SYSTEMS HAVE ACTIVATED! USE YOUR SHRINKING POWERS TO SLOWLY SNEAK THROUGH! GO BACK ONE SPACE.

A CENTIPEDE STRIKES! YOU CAN DEFEAT IT, BUT IT'LL SLOW YOU DOWN. GO BACK TWO SPACES.

ANT-MAN START

ANGRY ANT ATTACK! ANT-MAN IS ABLE TO EVADE THE INSECT — SKIP FORWARD TWO SPACES!

HITCH A RIDE ON THE BACK OF A FLYING ANT! ZIP FORWARD TWO SPACES.

FINISH

11 12 13 10 9 8 7 6 5 4 3 2 1

43

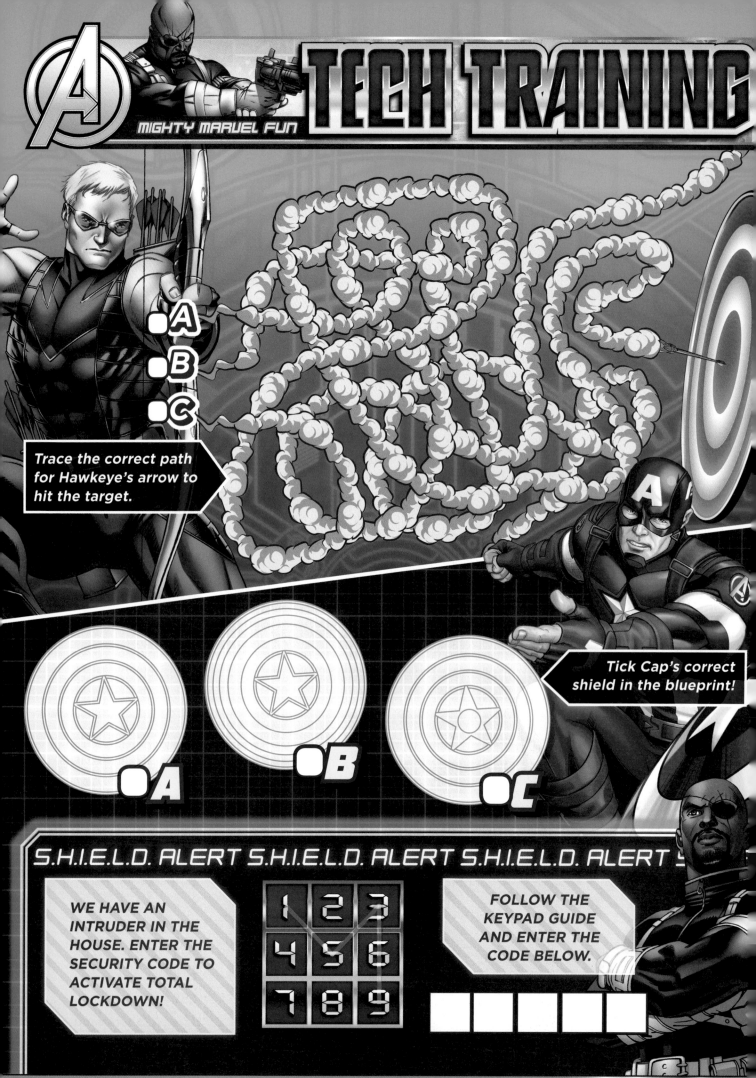

MIGHTY MARVEL FUN

A

B

C

Trace the correct path for Hawkeye's arrow to hit the target.

A

B

C

Tick Cap's correct shield in the blueprint!

S.H.I.E.L.D. ALERT S.H.I.E.L.D. ALERT S.H.I.E.L.D. ALERT S

WE HAVE AN INTRUDER IN THE HOUSE. ENTER THE SECURITY CODE TO ACTIVATE TOTAL LOCKDOWN!

1 2 3
4 5 6
7 8 9

FOLLOW THE KEYPAD GUIDE AND ENTER THE CODE BELOW.

the REPLACEMENTS
JOE CARAMAGNA WRITER
RON LIM ARTIST
SCOTT HANNA INKER
CARLOS LOPEZ COLORIST
VC's JC LETTERER
DARREN SHAN EDITOR
AXEL ALONSO EDITOR IN CHIEF
JOE QUESADA CHIEF CREATIVE OFFICER
DAN BUCKLEY PUBLISHER
ALAN FINE EXECUTIVE PRODUCER
AVENGERS CREATED BY STAN LEE & JACK KIRBY
JUST AS I SUSPECTED.
ATTENTION, ALL PERSONNEL! AVENGERS TOWER IS UNDER ATTACK--

--BY THE *CHITAURI!*

KRANG!

ZRKK

THWAK

KRAKK

WATCH YOUR LANGUAGE.

CHK!

THEY'VE TAKEN OUT OUR POWER.

IF WE'RE TO HOLD THE TOWER AGAINST THIS INVASION, WE NEED *ALL HANDS ON DECK--*

"--SO WHERE IS *TONY STARK?*"

THIS IS ONLY THE SECOND TIME I'VE EVER SNUCK INTO MY OWN HOME.

ONE TIME WHEN I WAS A KID, MY PARENTS WERE OFF IN *LISBON*--OR WAS IT *BUDAPEST?*--AND IT WAS JUST ME AND EDNA, MY NANNY OF THE WEEK.

IT WAS WAY PAST CURFEW AND EDNA SLEPT LIKE A *BEAR*, SO SHE NEVER HEARD ME CLIMB IN THROUGH THE BATHROOM WINDOW.

SHE WAS A NICE LADY--AND MADE GREAT *PANCAKES*-- BUT SHE WAS NO SUBSTITUTE FOR DAD.

I WOULDN'T HAVE DARED TO TRY IT IF HE WERE HOME. HE WAS ALWAYS UP LATE WORKING AND COULD HEAR EVERY--

--THING.

WIDOW, THIS ISN'T ONE OF YOUR TRAINING SIMULATIONS, IS IT?

IT *CAN'T* BE, HAWKEYE. THE POWER'S DOWN IN THE WHOLE BUILDING. EVEN THE *BACKUP* SYSTEM ISN'T RUNNING.

THIS IS THE *REAL DEAL.*

CLAPP!

BRUMMMMMM!

WHOOOAA--

~AAAHHH!

KRMM!

TONY? WHEN DID YOU GET BACK?

JUST NOW. AND TO BE HONEST, YOUR IDEA OF A "WELCOME HOME" PARTY *STINKS.*

NOT EXACTLY DRESSED FOR COMBAT, ARE YOU?

ONE CAN'T EXACTLY SNEAK PAST AN *ALIEN ARMY* WEARING RED-AND-GOLD *BATTLE ARMOR*--

SO...

PART 2

OUR CHITAURI FRIENDS HACKED THE *DEFENSE SATELLITE BLOCKADE* I SET UP TO KEEP THEM CONFINED TO THEIR SECTOR IN SPACE.

SO I *SAW.*

I TRIED TO RESTORE IT, BUT YOUR TECHNOLOGY IS VERY DIFFERENT FROM THAT OF MY HOME KINGDOM OF *WAKANDA.*

I BET YOU'RE ALL HAPPY TO SEE ME *NOW.*

NONE MORE THAN *I.* THESE PAST FEW WEEKS, I HAVE SEEN THAT THE AVENGERS ARE BETTER WHEN EACH MEMBER PLAYS A SPECIFIC *ROLE.*

THE AVENGERS NEED *TONY STARK.* NOT SOME *SUBSTITUTE.*

NOW THAT YOU HAVE RETURNED, THE BLACK PANTHER MUST RETURN TO HIS SUBJECTS.

WELL? BRING YOUR DEFENSE BLOCK-Y WHATEVER BACK UP AND WE'RE GOOD TO GO.

IF I DO THAT NOW, THE *GIANT SHIP* HOVERING OVER THE CITY WILL BE *TRAPPED* HERE WITH US IN *OUR* SECTOR.

SO WHAT DO WE DO?

FORCE IT TO *RETREAT.*

T'CHALLA, BEFORE YOU GO, WHAT DO YOU SAY TO *ONE LAST MISSION?* I'LL EVEN LET YOU DO THE *HONORS...*

AVENG

Tony Stark is in the building! Help him out as he sneaks around Avengers Tower!

1. INTRUDERS!

The Chitauri are all over Avengers Tower! How many has the security system identified on the scanner? Count all of the times you see 'CHITAURI' - they may be hidden forwards backwards or diagonally.

C	H	I	T	A	U	R	I	T	C
I	R	U	A	T	I	H	C	C	H
D	O	J	K	C	J	O	P	V	I
A	O	R	T	H	K	A	R	J	T
K	D	G	R	I	G	Q	T	K	A
S	C	H	I	T	A	U	R	I	U
L	J	A	T	A	S	C	D	R	R
O	W	R	R	U	O	G	S	U	I
J	K	V	A	R	A	C	K	A	S
A	R	T	G	I	C	O	A	T	A
C	O	R	S	J	X	J	S	I	S
C	H	I	T	A	U	R	I	H	D
S	O	X	T	G	T	O	J	C	R

INPUT THE ANSWER HERE:

2. POWER SOURCE

>>>Begin the power-up sequence by selecting the correct circuit.>>>

START!
A.   B.   C.

3. LOW PROFILE

Hey it's dark in here! Tony can barely make out the shape of these guys. Are they Chitauri? Or Avengers?

Mark each box with an
A for Avengers or a
C for Chitauri.

PATH OF

MIGHTY MARVEL FUN

When Black Panther's not saving the world, he's protecting his home nation! Follow the hero through the gates of Wakanda on a journey to protect the most advanced country on Earth!

- A game for one to two players.
- You will need: a dice and some scissors (ask an adult to help you cut out the counters to the right)!
- Each player takes a turn to roll the dice, moving that number of spaces. Follow the instructions on the white spaces – the first to reach the finish can claim the title of the new Black Panther!

1. A WAKANDAN WELCOME!
To enter the gates of Wakanda, roll an even number. If it's 1, 3 or 5, Bast the Panther Goddess will not let you pass!

START

2.

3.

4. COMBAT TRAINING WITH CAPTAIN AMERICA!
Roll a **3, 4 or 5** to land the finishing blow and progress to the next square!

5.

6. ROOFTOP PATROL!
Your tour of the Wakandan skyline takes longer than expected. Don't move this turn and progress 3 steps on the next go!

7.

8. PROWLING PANTHER!
Night falls on Wakanda, and your stealth suit's working like a charm!
Roll a **2 or a 4** to sculk through to square 11!

9.

10. A CHALLENGER APPEARS!
A contender for the Black Panther mantle demands to battle you!
Progress to square 12 next turn!

THE PANTHER

14. ULTIMATE UPGRADE!
Wakanda's head scientists have honed your suit's sensors, leading to a leaner, meaner Black Panther! If you roll a **1-4** next turn, move forward double the amount!

15.

16.

17.

13.

12.

18. AVENGERS ANTI-GRAY ADVENTURE!
Exposure to anti-gravity has reversed the numbers on your dice! Roll a 1 to move forward 6 spaces – roll a 6 to move forward 1! Otherwise, miss a go!

19.

FINISH

20.

25.

24. ULTIMATE DOOM!
Doctor Doom has invaded looking for rare vibranium, and it's your job to repel the villain!

Roll a 5 to disable his armour – nothing else will defeat him!

11.

21.

22. TECHNO TROUBLE!
A techno-virus has infected your people... Use your suit's upgrades to save the day!

Roll a 2 or a 3 to calibrate your feral frequencies and move on one space, or miss a go!

23.

SAY WHAT?!

WHAT HAPPENS WHEN ODIN AND THOR CONFRONT EACH OTHER? YOU DECIDE! FILL IN THE BLANKS WITH ANY OF THE WORDS BELOW AND CREATE A COOL CONVERSATION!

WORD MANIA

"ARGHHHH MY SON, YOU HAVE _____ ME AGAIN! WHY DO YOU FAIL ME SO?"

- ANGERED
- SHOCKED
- DELIGHTED

"FATHER NOOOO! I AM JUST AFRAID OF BEING WORTHLESS WITHOUT MY _____..."

- HELMET
- HAIR
- HAMMER

"NONSENSE! YOU ARE A TRUE WARRIOR. YOU MUST GROW UP AND BE A REAL _____."

- CHICKEN
- GOD
- MAN

"BUT HOW WILL I EVER BECOME AS _____ AS YOU? I LOOK UP TO YOU, FATHER..."

- POWERFUL
- HANDSOME
- SMELLY

"ONLY TIME WILL TELL... START NOW AND WORK YOUR WAY UP TO THE _____."

- KITCHEN
- HEAVENS
- TOP

"YOU ARE RIGHT. I WILL STOP BEING A COWARD AND CONQUER MY _____!"

- FEARS
- LOOKS
- TROUBLES

8 FIGHTING FISTS

22 SPELL BOUND

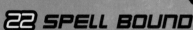

SURRENDER

STEPHEN

23 CITY SEARCH

24-25 ROCKET'S WORKSHOP

YOU CAN'T GET THE STAFF:
3579

MISS ME?:   TARGET INCOMING:
C   CENTAURI CRUISER

26 ATTACK OF THE GIANTS

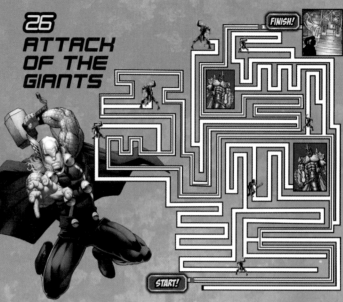

FINISH!

START!

40-1 EYE SPIDEY

44 TECH TRAINING

1-C, 2-A, 3-15369

56-57 AVENGERS TOWER

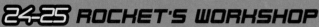

START!

C   A

C

C

A   A

7